# SEQUOIA

## Poems of Eternity

Elizabeth Anne Hin

Copyright © 2018 Elizabeth Anne Hin
All Rights Reserved

Illustrations Copyright © 2018 by Cynthia L. Kirkwood

Editing, Design, & Composition by Sarla V. J. Matsumura

Library of Congress Control Number: 2018946510

ISBN-13: 978-0692106464
ISBN-10: 0692106464

Printed in the United States of America

Published by Issa Press
Austin, Texas

# DEDICATION

To Joseph Alexander Brodsky
John David Gabriel
Blaine Richard Glass
Andre Haridev Gobius

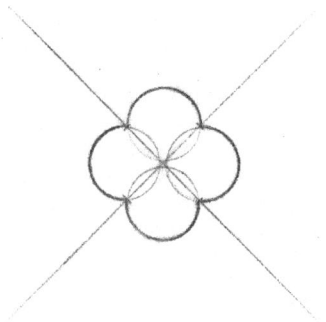

## CONTENTS

| | |
|---|---|
| Clothed in Trees | 1 |
| One | 3 |
| The Shepherd | 7 |
| Flame | 11 |
| And | 15 |
| Benevolent | 17 |
| Night | 19 |
| Toujours | 21 |
| Uncle Michael's Niece | 25 |
| Feather | 27 |
| Beyond | 67 |
| Ever and Always | 73 |
| Beckoning | 79 |
| Haridev | 81 |
| Autumn Day | 83 |
| Seventy | 87 |
| He Awaits Her | 89 |
| Shawl | 97 |
| The Country of Roses | 101 |
| White Flower | 103 |
| The One | 105 |

# CLOTHED IN TREES

The men
Of my life

Are clothed in trees

Bark is their armor

Their skin

Which knows

There is no
Warrior

Only

A
Son
Saint
Father
Brother
Uncle
Companion
Spouse
Colleague

Sap

Life's blood

Their
Flow

Of seasons

Rooting
Sprouting
Branching
Leafing
Budding
Fruiting
Seeding

These

Are

My Husband
My Brothers
My Son

They
Are
Life

There
Is
No
War.

# ONE

In a row
They were there
Silver Birches
One, two, three, maybe four
Silver
Trunks
As
Soft
Grey
Tawny

As
A
Dove
Or two or three or maybe four
Doves
Would be

And
Green
Like
The
Essence
Of

A
First
Day
Of
Spring

Straight, tall

And then
Further

Along
That
Country
Road
There were more
Maybe
One hundred
Years
Older
Silver
Deep
Mottled
Horizontal
Marks
Of cold
Winters
Of
Much
Peace
And
War
Argument
Toward
War
And
Then
Peace

Respite
From
Beyond
Argument

And then
Further
Along

There
Were
More
Many
A young
Grove
Of
Many

Beyond
All
War
One
Tree
Of
Life
Not two or three or maybe four
But
One
A Grove
Created
Of
Many
And
Of
Love

One
Holy
Grove
One
Family
One
Tree

Silver
Birch

# THE SHEPHERD

I.
And

On
This
Day

You
Are

Father
Shepherd

Three

Rest
In your silence

Strength
Blessing
Stoic grace
Diligent
Disciplined
Yearning
Striving
Work
Accomplishments
Tasks

Your tireless

Humility
Honor
Tenderness

True goodness

And
In
What is not known

Every River
They must forge

You have forged

Into eternity
In your faith for them

II.
May our
Children
Follow the bridge

Of all wisdom

And

Love
You who are their Father
Truly

Over all rivers
Under all rivers
Through all rivers
That have ever been
Are
Will ever be

Swollen in flood
Torrential
Raging
Drought ridden
Dry
Toxic

Cleansed
Potable

All rivers

Your soul
A veritable
River man of God

III.
Carrying them
Three

Fording all waters
In faith alive
As
Father

As
Home for their
Safe souls
In you.

# FLAME

O flame

Of God
Of Heaven
On Earth

I pray

O spring

Of Divine
Flow
Of grace
And meaning

Of life

O stone

Firmament
Upon
Whom

I stand

Offering
In innocence
Her dance

O
Vast
Sky

Of this
Milky Way adorned

I breathe

Hopefully yearned
Faithfully tended
Lovingly named
Earth
Earth

Home

Not yet

No

Heaven
Is home

And

This
Waystation

This

This

Is homesick

I
Am

She prays
Remember

Be
The
Flame
Spring
Firmament

Alight
Nourished
Grounded
Breathing
Breathing
I say breathing

Alive
Blessed

Whole
Real

Remember

Let us dance
We are prayer.

Young Woman
Young Women
My Sister
Our Daughter
Let us pray.

# AND

And
On
The
Highest
Levels
One
He
She
That
That Great One
The
Dharmakya
The Clear Light
Of
Reality
The Pure
Perfect
Unmanifest
Manifest
Beyond
All
So
Vast
And unable
To
Be
Named
Though
We try
Strive
And
Honor
With our
Naming

There
Is
All
Of
Only
Goodness
Caused
Borne
Birthed
Tended
Shepherded
Home
Into
That
Of
That
Becoming
That

If you do not know that goodness
Are not that goodness
Realized
Yet
You are not there yet
Keep going
Keep on
Toward

And

# BENEVOLENT

You
Benevolent
Man
Son
Father
Cousin
Counselor
Sage
Philosopher
Physician
Scientist
Researcher
Rancher
My great love
Shoulders affixed
To the wings
Of all great Angels
Feet treading this blessed Earth
Arms outreaching in all ways and always
To fulfill
A path
Of no harm
To any
And
All
Of
Healing
Earnest
Giving
Sharing
Bequeathing

In
All that you face
Represent
Regard
Respect
You become
As
Of Mercy
Son
Beloved
Of
God.

For Jdg

# NIGHT

In this night sky

I fly

Desert
Ocean
Mountain
Vale

This man
Woman
All people
One tribe

A poem

Of blossom

Paradise.

# TOUJOURS

Across
The
Broad
Beach
Soft
At
The
Sea
Azure
Blue
Through
The
Trees
Tawny
And
Green
Palms
There
Is
Light
Of
All
Colours
Holy
And
Beautiful

Chagall
Lived
There
Matisse
Renoir, nearby
Inspired
Beloved

This
Place
Of
Fragonard
My
Orange Blossom
Perfume
Fragrance
Of
Grace

White wine
In
Tall glasses
Beneath
Baccarat
Crystal
Chandelier
Of
The Negresco
Palace
Crystal
Created
For
A
Czar
Killed
In
Revolution

A
Century
Later
Now
Lighting
The
Triage

For
Bodies
Red
With
Blood
Attacked
Here
In
Provence

We
Remember
Them
All
Souls
Of
Light
Czar
And
Czarina
Revolutionaries
Monsieur
Negresco
Of
Romania
Historic
Stars
And
Citizens
Of
France
Of
Our
World

As
Humanity
Walks
In
Light
Of
All Colours

Along the Promenade
The promenade of the English
Not
The promenade of sorrow
But the walk
Of Liberty
Fraternity
Brotherhood
Always
Nice,
Toujours
France.

For the Family of the Colombe d'Or,
Saint Paul de Vence

# UNCLE MICHAEL'S NIECE

She is running
In the sun
There are vines
Almost full
With draping
Grape
Clusters
Pinot
Soon
They
Will perfume
The very air
Atmosphere
With their ripe fruit
Turning to wine
She
Almost
Three
Sacred
Decades
Turning to wine
A vintage
Of God
Ruby
In her soul
Clear
In aspiration and faith
Viscous
In her rich complex depth
Of being
Fruity
In her laugh
Filled with turning to wine
Before God
Serving humanity

The environment
Of grapevines
Orchards
Vineyards
And people
Hawks
To all creatures
Her heart's meaning
Is a veritable joy
Of Heaven's harvest
Midsummer
She runs
In
The fields
Of the Lord.

For Kirsten Elise Gabriel

# FEATHER

I.
He brought to me
A
Ring
It was
The feather
Of a
Jay
Verdant
Blue
Color
Of
The sky
White
Of
All clouds
The black marks
Of the internal
Light
Of my
Mother's womb
Heart
My
Father's semen
Seed
Of
All
That is
Of
All colors
My feathered
Body

The spine
Of the
Feather's
Quill
So strong
Supple
Resilient
As my soul
Within
This form
The tip
Of the Feather
Having
Brushed the air
With
Purpose
Joy
And
Life
A
Thousand
Times
A thousand

Before
Shedding
To
Grow
Anew

A
Feather
He
Brought
To me

A ring
Of
God
Not
Bound
Upon
My finger
But from his strong hand
I so trust
Into mine
From below our
Beloved
Pecan tree
Right here
At his
Home
Home
Of many
Birds
Three
Nestlings
Of
Him
And
This
One.

II.
Then he brought
Another
Jewel
A ring
Not a ring
Of
But
A
Ring
He stacked wood
Men cut chopped
Drove brought to him
Placed
And he stacked split and carried each day
Autumn Winter Early Spring
In when cool cold
To our hearth
And a flame
As
A ring of God
Blessed me then
In his love
And us
In His love.

III.
At
The
Shore
We
Walked
Late
Afternoon
The
Day
We
Arrived
First
We
Bicycled
From
That
Tender
Olden
House
Of
A
Famed
Family
Inn
Now
Let
To people
Folks
Like us
In beauty
Great kindness
Dignity
Vacation
And
Rest

Many
Eastern
Traditions
Of
America
As
Those
Of
My
Birth
Family

We
Pedaled
Upon
Sturdy
Bicycles
Beneath
Spanish Moss
Bridal veiling
Coastal Oaks
On our
Way
And
Then
We
Found
An
Impasse
Before
Us
A
Couple
Newly
Wed

At
That
Splendid
Home
Just
The
Day
Before
Now
Crouched
Rather
Dramatically
Beside
Their
Open
Jeep
And
Driver
Their
Marriage
Challenged
The
Driver's
Face
Distressed

Searching
For
The
Extravagant
Ring
Gift
Of
A
Husband

Of
A
Man's
Promise
To a
Woman
Before
God
And
All
The
Universe
Known
And
Unknown
Lost
In
Dunes
Just
Before
The
Beach
His
Betrothed's
Opulently
Adorned
Fingers
Rather
Desperate
In
The
Sand

Her
Wedding
Nails
Would
Now
Be
Ruined
This
Was
Not
Funny
She
Continued
Her
Fingertips
Had
Been
Ornamented
In
The
Finest
Treatments
At
An
Expensive
Renowned
Spa
And
That
He
Well
He
Had
Better
Find
It

His
Fault
Already
All
Ruined

One
Day
After
Her
Promised
Had
Placed
In
Prayer
And
All
That
He
Was
Has
Is
Shall
Ever
Become
Hoped
Pledged
Before
God
Upon
The
Venus
Finger

Of
His
Intended's
Left
Hand
That
Day
Before

We
Were
Still
Home
In Texas
Then
That
Day
Before
And
She
Said
With
A
Voice
For
No
Groom
No
Man
Nor
Woman
She
Said
It is worth
A day
After
I do

So
Much
At least
Twenty~five
Thousand
Maybe forty
He
Responded
Babe
The insurance
She
Answered
Maybe
And
Then
In
The
Earth
Of
Which
It
Is
Made
He
Found
Their
Metal
And
Stone
Symbol
He
Tried
To
Place
Again
On her
Hand

Finger
Truth
Pledged
Now
Blessed
With
Sky
O island
Waves
O island
All
Promise
O island
And
She
Would
Have
None
Of
It

Said
No
Put
It
In
Your
Pocket
My
Manicure
Is
Ruined
I
Broke
A
Nail
And

Don't
Lose
It
This
Time
His
Fault
Too
Even
Having
Fallen
Off
Her
Finger
That
First
Challenge
His
Fault
Even
If
Never
Lost ever
Again
His
Fault
No
Vow
Holy
Here
In
Her
Today

I
Could
Not
Imagine
His
Hurt
For
Grooms
Are
As
Sensitive
As
Brides
He
In
And out
Of the
Doghouse
This
First
Day
Of
Their
Marriage
Every
Day
I
Hope
Not
Surely
Not

Silently
I
Asked
Heaven's
Blessing

For
Them
Said
Perhaps
One
Might
Regard
Their
Rings
Hands
Wedding
Lives
Souls
And
All
Of
Us
Blessed
As
If
A
Native American
Tribal
Sacred
Elder
Of
This
Place
Or
Elsewhere
In
Our
Nation
World
Had
Offered
Ceremony

Through
All
Elements
Of
This
Place
Now
In
Life

My
Darling
And
I
Turned
Quietly
To
One
Another
I
Sighed
As I will do
And we
Headed
On
We saw
No one
Else
Glad
Sweet
Solitude
Of
A
Couple
Precious
And
True

Beach
Vast
Expanse
Grand
Vistas
Sweeping
Before
Us
Like
Nothing
I
Had
Ever seen
Fragrant
Soft
Wind
Scent
Of
Sea Oats
And
Grasses
Cypress
And
Oak
Silken
Crystalline
Soil
Wrought
Into
Sands
Perfect
Pure
At
This
Water's
Edge

Of
Salted
Air
Pastel
Tones
Of
Sky
Effusive
Clouds
Such
Beauty
Blessing
Every
Sense

Our walk
Open
To the
East
Sea
Of
All
Branches
Of
Our
Ancestral
Families
His
And
Mine
Atlantic

My Darling
Striding
Quite
Far
As he will do
Philosophizing
With eternity
And
Such
Real
Joyful
And
True
Regarding
Meaning
Everywhere
And
Always

He
Headed
To the North
Perhaps
A mile
And back
To me
As
I
Turned
To the South
I
Saw
Something
In the
Shallows

At
The very
Edge
Of
That
Splendid
Broad
Shore
And
Walked
Toward
The ring
Of
All
Waters
Ring
Formed
By
All
Waters
Of
All
Our
World
Surrounding
A
Ring
Of land
Upon
Which
We
Visited
Precious
Barrier island
With
Wild
Horses

Descended
From
Those
Of
Spanish
Ships
Wrecked
In
Storms
No
Sailors
To
Survive
Only
Splendid
Horses
Saved
By grace
Their
Gorgeous
Descendants
Free
In small
Herds
Content
So
Deeply
Loved
Living
Totem
Of this
Place
Upon
This
Ring
Of land

And
Past
Shallow
Tide
Pools
Stepping
Into
The
Softest
Surf
At
The
Ring
Of
The
One
Great
Ocean
Of
Our
Earth
Here
Two shells
Whelks
Nestled
In
God
Facing one another
One slightly smaller
Diminutive
One beautifully
Handsomely
Formed
Proportioned
Both
Foot tips
Facing shoreward

Shell openings
Heavenward
The direction
From which
That Great One
Brought
To us
This ring
Of two shells
This promise
Of two like creatures
On our broad beach
Undisturbed
Our ring
Our wedding ring

And
Gathering
Our
Bicycles
To ride
Back
Here
Came
People
In
Another
Jeep
Asking
If
Folks
Might
Like
A
Pleasant
Ride
Back

People
At the beginning
With lost
Found rings
And
People
At the end
Ringing us
Home
In loving
Welcome

With
Our
Whelk shells
Ever after
At
Our
Bedroom
Chest
A ring
Made of sea foam
Vistas
Horizons
Colors
Of Heaven
Breezes
Of
God
A ring
Blessing
This man and woman
In grace.

IV.
Our
Cherished
'Waltz Across Texas'
Actually
Ernest Tubbs
Song
Chosen
As
Our
Ring
Of music
Dale
Fiddles
On
This night
For us
And for all
At
Mr. Pyle's
Stampede
So
Touched
To
Hear him
See him
Play
Smile
Sing
Be
Live
We heard
The
Fiddle
Could
It
Be

It
Was
Him
The
Fiddler of God

Ten years ago
We heard
The
Now
Late
Ray Price
Symphony Hall
Classic suit
And tie
Stunning
Singular
Performance
Singing
Hallowed
Meyerson
Dallas
His home town
He so loved
Deeply
Moving
To us
Voice
Musicians

And then
The
Fiddler of God
Dale
Lifted
His
Instrument

To
A
Shoulder
And
Moving
Like
The
Ocean
Played
Like
The
Veritable winds
Of Jesus' blessing
We had
Never
Heard
Seen felt or been moved
By anything
Like it
Before
Or
Since

That
Next month
The fiddler of God
Entered
My Beloved's office
For medical wisdom
And care
My Beloved
Entrusted to me
In prayer
As he does
Rare times
To pray for this man
This one

Our fiddler of God
How could he
Have played
That
Hallowed hall
Like an angel
In such pain
Such music
Such a soul
For ten years
I pray
For him
His Family
Work
Life
And several times
Each week
My Beloved and I think of his music
That night
Ten years
Ago
God's fiddler
Wafting in upon our souls, hearts, and lives
In Grace, meaning
And God's own joy

Within myself
Ten years ago
I chose
That
If ever we married
Our wedding
Ring
Ring
Of song
Would be
Asked

Of one
Music
A gift
If I could
Find
A way
I would seek
God's fiddler
And
Ask of him
Wherever
We
Were
To wed
Would he come
Just him
Surprise
My Texan
In
Playing
God's fiddler

A little Bob Wills
A little ballad
Or two
A fine piece of mountain
Prairie or
Historic fiddle
'How Great Thou Art'
For all four
Of our beloved
Late parents
And
Or
Any other Hymn
Of the Lord
Or two

This Fiddler
Being
Familiar
At ease
With
Songs
Of grace

And
Our
Ernest Tubbs'
'Waltz Across Texas'
For my Beloved
And me

I knew
The fiddler of God
Would remember
My Beloved
From merciful care
Of medicine and soul
And now love
And my Beloved would
Wed
The
One
True
God's fiddler
Ringing him
In song
Ringing us
In
His
Fiddler's grace.

For Dr. John D. Gabriel
and Dale Morris, Junior

V.
Husband
Gifting
Feathers
Of
Sapphire
And
Topaz
All
Beauty
All
Grace

Husband
Of sunlight
Moonlight
Too
We
Are
Ringed
By oceans
Upon islands
And
Continents
Over
All
The Earth
Beneath
Milky Way
Pleiades
Northern Lights
Dawn
Over
Lakes

From
Crater
To
Keuka
Nights
By
Seas
From
Iceland
To
Milford
Journeys
To
Mountains
From
Rocky
To
Andes
Life
At
The
Prairies
Of
Your
Home
And
Southern
Grace

All
Of
God
Your
Love

A bouquet
Of
All
Wildflowers
Found
In English
Fields
With
Splendid
Pheasants
Long
Ago
Introduced
By
Romans
Pairs
Of
Glorious
Birds
At
The
Ancestral
Lands
Of
Your
Family
And
At
Their
Heritage
To
You
My
Stoic
Texan

In
All
Joy
And
Gravitas
At
Home
Your
Home
Your
Family
Ranch
Your
Mother's
Bluebonnets
And
Flowers
And
At
The
Home
Of
My
Grandmothers'
Northern
Queen Anne's Lace
And
So many
I love
Of
Color
And
Leaf
Petal
And
Stem

Your
Rings
Of
Life
Gift
To me
A song
Pure
As
A
Ruby
Of
The
Old
Testament
Bringing
Tears
To
Your
And
My
Eyes
As
The
Fiddler
Of
God
Waltzes
Our
Souls

To
The
Dance
Of
Our
Parents'
Blessing
Upon
Us

At
Hearthside
Shepherding
Three
Precious
Children
Now
Grown
Strong
And
In
Our
Faith
And
Hope
We
Hold
Them
To
Become
That
Living
Grace
Always
God's
Love
Incarnate

Snapping
Your fingers
To
Our Tobe
His
Blue
Heeler
Howl
And
Furry
Nestle
Beside
Us
Nothing
He
Loves
Like
Being
With
You

Paying
Bills
Late
At
Night
Writing
Charts
Of
Patients
Faithfully
Each
Day
A jewel
Brought me
Of your
Goodness

Your fidelity
And trust
In what
Is right
What is true
What is real

Blessed
By
A feather
My finger
Ringed
In
The
Emerald
Of
Our
Life
On
Earth
The
Diamond
Light
Of
Eternity

In
The
Pearl
Dawn
The peace
Of Doves
Morning breast
Of Robins
Sweet song
Of Wrens
At our back doorstep

Region
Of Mockingbirds
Marriage
Of two souls
Two lives
One ring

He brought to me
A
Ring
It was
The feather.

For Jdg,
    B

# BEYOND

There were men of war
Men of weapons
Women, too
And
There was Brodsky
When asked
And where did you get your words
'I believe it came from God'
Assigned
To Siberia
He found
A
Cabin
The chopping
Splitting
Of wood
Wind
In the trees
Spring water
Firelight
Northern Lights
Four English books
Exile
And
For
Me
Who
Loved him always
No weapons
Could name us
Only our love
Of God
He, She, That beyond all
Weapons
Beyond all argument and harm

In our poets' world
Real true eternal
His heart broken
He died
Somewhat
Early
No
Return
To Russia
Allowed him
By men
And women of war
So
I journeyed
To
His
Russia
His
Saint Petersburg
For him
Walked
With my cane
Where my Josef
Loved
To
Walk
His body
At rest
Now
On an isle
At the waters
Of Venice
Son of his early love
Daughter of his late love

Held
In
Our
Promise to God
That they might
Be
Remembered of God
From
The
Same source
As
Was
Born
His
Poetry

There were men of war
Women, too
And
There was Neruda
Ode himself
To the Earth
And all beauty
Faith
Passion
And
Care
Writing
Of love
The Sea
I took a recording
A reading
Of
His poems
And from
That
Voice

Resonant
Sublime
Juan Gabriel
His
First years
Learned words
Beside his
Family
Mother
Young uncle and aunts the
Grandmother
And Grandmother's
Shepherd
Farmer
Lover
Protector
Of
Them
All
Etched
In
Juan's
Soul
His
First years
As he
Now
Turns
Eight
2016
Poets' world
Of Neruda
Brodsky
And
Me

Words of
Soil
Tree trunk
Toil
Heart
Quest
And
Faith
Beyond all argument and harm
Beyond war
Beyond,
Poets,
Here.

# EVER AND ALWAYS

On my birthday
Spontaneously
I prayed
Thought of God
The numinous reality
I experience ever
And always

And
World peace
Autumn leaves
Places
I have been privileged
To know

Y'upik Eskimo lands
Of tundra
And grace
Intimacy of
Family there
Teaching me
How to be
With honor
And
Survival
Always and ever

Hiking to
And from
Mount Everest Base
Kala Pattar
Carrying all of my own
Equipment and food
Three and one half weeks
With three companions
It was very hard
And perfect
Rhododendron forests
In full bloom
For
So many miles
At the tree line
Taller than humans
Filled with late Spring
Himalayan blossoms

Russia
Kazan
Saint Petersburg
Where
People traveled
The Trans Siberian
From the border at Mongolia
From Moscow
And the fields of the Ukraine
That we might meet
For conference
And wise counsel
To help
Others

All who might need us
For a day
Year
A life
Of counsel
At thresholds
Of
Conflict
Confusion
Non~permission
Or despair

I walked the stairway
To the Sakharov apartment
Homage
To one
And his wife
Who helped
Counsel
Our whole world
Beyond nuclear war

And my Brodsky
Of the Silver Birch forests
Church candles
And
Such love
That my whole world
Burns with the flame
Always and ever

The lake where my Father
Young
Constructed a cottage
With his hands
While my Mother carried me
Within her tender body

And my now late
Elder brother awaited
His sister
Such love
Waves lapping at the shore
Grapevines on hillsides
Willow
Elm
Ash
Cottonwood
Too
Rounded slate stones forming a shoreline
And the Seneca Iroquois soul
All about us
Always and ever

My younger brother
Tending home hearth now
And France with such light
Aesthetics
Sentiment
Freedom and
Tradition
Plane Trees
Perfumes
Bread and
Such love
My breath becomes still
In quiet gratitude
Remembering this

And a Lake in Canada
Louise
Tears flowing from these eyes
At such beauty

And a lake
In England
Windermere
Ever
And
Always

And a great friend
Twin
To
This soul
Ever
And Always

And a Family
So blessed.

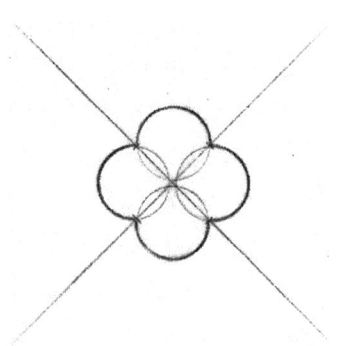

# BECKONING

A great swan
Arose
From
The blessed lake
Wings risen
To Heaven
Eyes
To eternity
Her heart
Fought
With
No one
Only
Knew
Fells and hollows
Brooks and waters
Of Grace
And goodness
Studied
Only that
Which is Holy
And right

She knows
The way Home
And calls
Come, come
Now.

# HARIDEV

And what
Shall
I say to you
Man of God
Man of faith
Hands forged
Of Heaven's will
Splinters,
Stain, paint
Calloused, worn skin
Dust of Earth
Tender brow
Blue eyes
Of such grace

No one
Can see
Know
Hear
Touch
Or understand
Your love
Resounding
Throughout
All time

As,
Covered
By your
Mother's
Tender blanket
You pray

For everyone
Every man
Woman
And child

And
Juan
Jesus
Your child
Of your heart.

Here, son
Live
As do I
And you will be free
Not crucified
Blue sky
Fox and bird
Deer and cloud
Chaparral and limestone

All our Earth
Son
Our home
Now
I have built it
For us.

For Andre Haridev Gobius

# AUTUMN DAY

On the day
Of your funeral
There was
A Night Heron
Complex creature
Of shadow and light
Like you
Quiet
Contemplating
Beneath a
Large Pine
You
Laid to rest
This morn
At a pair
Of splendid
Live Oaks
Songbirds hymning you
Grandchildren, too

At the waterside
He was
Still
Resolute
Content
Filled with
Great meaning
As
Beneath Sun,
Moon
And Stars
He rested
After flying
After fishing

Bustle
Of the city
All
About him
Undisturbed
He dwelt
In mystery
Of grace
As some
Timeless icon
Of reverie in nature
Reverence in faith
Blessing in aspiration
Fulfillment in love

Incomprehensibly handsome
Free
Fulfilled
On green grass
Under blue sky
White tufted face
With dark markings
Magnificent
Black
Green
Deepest blue
How
Might we say
Such a color
Night
As
In how
This Heron received
His name
Or Heaven

Where you have ascended
Now
And always
Forever
As your Persimmons ripen
This perfect
Brilliant
Autumn day.

For Charles Ray McClure

# SEVENTY

Her hair
Is
Silver
Now
And
Beautiful
As
Is
She
Eyes
Steady
Blue
As
A
Sapphire
Dedicated
To
Truth
This soul
Her heart
Full
Of freedom
Of care
Love
Dedication

Poppies
And
So very
Many flowers
Blooming
Just as
Does she
In God
And
Everywhere,
Seventy.

# HE AWAITS HER

He awaits her
She prays
For
Mankind
Humanity
Humankind
All creatures
And the creation
Which is
Home
Here
Owls
In
Trees
Whales
Below
Waves
On her knees
Mass
At
Beloved
Saintes Maries de la Mer
At
The gilded Vatican
Westminster Abbey
Lutheran
Chapel
Thingvellir
Communion
Of
Bread
And leaves
Beneath trees
Lingonberries

With
Farmers
In
Their kitchens
Friesian cake
At their porticos
Beside their
Beloved fields
Places of worship
All

Synagogues

Beyond
All
And
Any
Names
One
Might
Say
To
Name
Heaven

Temples

Mosques

Beyond
Any
And
All
Swords
That
Mercy
Be

No
Swords
Only
Mercy
For
All

Shinto
Forest
Shrines
Of Kami
Everywhere
Silver Birches
Of the Sami
Of Russian
Shamans
And
Saints
Wonder Workers
And
Laborers

Stupas pointed
Starward
Toward
Buddha's
Remembrance
Flowers
Placed
Before
The spires
And
Offered
Before
His Enlightenment
Tathagata

And
Also
Trays
Of
Marigolds
Incense
And
Butter
Burning
Alight
With
Cotton
Wick
In
Tiny lamps
As Puja
To gods and gods and gods
To goddesses and goddesses and goddesses
Of Hindu
Men and women
Praying
As have
Their Mothers
Their Fathers
And
Their Children

At
Universities
Praying
As did
Rilke
Aristotle
Mozart
Chinese man
Hopi woman
King Asoka
And
Pericles
Wife of Persia

As Hesiod
Wrote
Springtime
The Cattle
And
Autumn
The Harvest
And Homer
Perceiving
Beyond all
Sight
Reciting
Heaven
To be
The
Loom
Of the Wife
Tended
By her
Faith
Unfailing
In God

Daughter
Of
All Muses
As her
Husband
Sailed
Hell
Earth
And
Back
To
Home
Argos
Protecting
Her
As
She
Tended
Heaven's
Loom
Argos
And
She
Awaiting
Him

Youth
Sometimes
To a God
Name
Place
Way

Sometimes now
To a
Vastness
Of Space
Time
Eternity
Aspiration
No gods now
No deities
No
Scrolls
Sutras
Torahs
Bibles
Mosques
Holy books
Sacred texts
Scriptures
Their own egos
And wardrobes
Too important for
That
The Void empty
Full
Unfulfilled
They believe
They do not believe

Let us
Pray
Practice
Feed the sheep
Horses
Chickens
Goats
Dog
Cats
Birds
Please, too
Always
Make certain
The
Animals
Are
Watered
The cattle
First thing
He awaits her
Tobe
At his feet
Eternal grace
At his side
Heaven
On Earth

For Jdg
  B

# SHAWL

I am

Clothed

In grace

For
Although

They

Wear
Dresses

My sisters

As
They

Pray
Walk
And

Turn

In life

Wear

Flowers

On their shoulders

Upon their collarbones
Tossed
For

Warmth
Protection
And
Beauty

Over

Their arms

Upon

Their backs

Sometimes

And

Across
Their breasts

Shawls

Of tulips
Irises
And
Roses
Honeysuckle
Jasmine
Lotus
Peony

Every kind of bloom

Lilacs
Fragrant

Lilies

And
Small buds

Of Wildflowers
The blossoms of God's signature
His ways
Tossed upon the fields of His Earth

Everywhere scattered in seed and promise

Throughout His world

Of grace

To be realized

And
My Mother's
Orchids

Ever
In
Living
Prayer
And
Ways

Toward the one
For the one
In all people
Everyone
Everywhere
And always.

# THE COUNTRY OF ROSES

In the country of roses
She is a root
Embracing
The
Earth
Embraced by

In the country of roses
She is a shoot
Turned
Heavenward
Addressing
The Lord
'Sir'

In the country of roses
She is a stem
Arched
Into grace
Becoming a dancer
Of wind
Rain
Sun
Moon
Stars
Turned skyward

In the country of roses
She is a leaf
Patterned
As if
A veritable
Tree of life
In miniature form

Diminutive
And tender
Carrying a
Small butterfly
Resting
Upon her
In refuge
In sanctuary
To pray
As life itself

In the country of roses
She is a bud
All hope
And promise

In the country of roses
She blooms

In the country of roses
She has
Turned
Turned into
Turned to
Become
Perfume
The fragrance
Of God's
Name
Every petal holy
And real
Fulfilled
One rose.

For Camille Adams Helminski

# WHITE FLOWER

On this day toward your death
Carolina Jessamine, Confederate Jasmine
Blooms yellow on the vine
At our bedroom in Dallas, at our bedroom
  in Austin
Flowers in bud, and lily~shaped blossoms
Yellow as your mind, intelligent as a
  goddess
The color of Saraswati

On the morning of
In the black deep dark, the very middle of
  the night
I awake, and with your Mother in Heaven
See you Home, so sad, so holy, and
  so beautiful

At oranged Dawn two mornings before
Just outside our Dallas door
The very first Robin of Spring,
  red~breasted, glorious
Perches on that yellow~flowering vine
And this Northeastern girl is fulfilled
The sweet bird's chest tenderly rusted
  scarlet as
Your Vermont Maple leaves
  mid~Autumn

Mid~afternoon, our vast Lonestar
  Sky
Opens blue as the doorway your soul
  now enters
Deep sky ~ Bluebonnets stand in the same
  threshold
All over Texas, blooming your pathway

A holy Grail's bouquet God has chosen
As if only for you, or rather
For your prayers ~ your prayers for
   everyone
Bluebonnets everywhere

While in your beloved Maine, snowmelt
   nourishes snowdrops
Sweetest white flower of your beloved New
England pressing up through
   the Earth
And curled tendrils of fern unfurling soon,
   too, on the forest floor

Not until after you are gone
Will the many greens be here
Of grasses, leaves, lichen and such
Except in the constant Balsam Pines
Wind weeping through them, crying for
   you
Through their soft needles God's own
   tears
Through the Atlantic Coastal, Cape,
   Island and inland valley breezes
Of your life, your holy life, your good life

Wise, tender, fierce, dedicated,
Nuanced, humorous, active, loyal
Wishing only that which is noble and true
Real and virtuous toward everyone
Adorned in your rainbow of all hues
Woman of light
Woman of God

For Margo W. MacLeod
and her Family

# THE ONE

The One from whom we come
Which we are
To realize
To remember
To serve
In Him

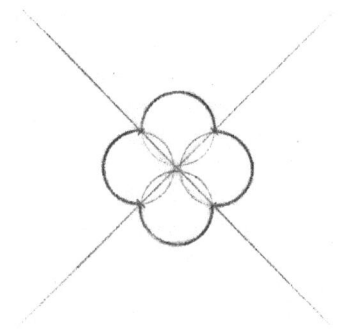

## ABOUT THE AUTHOR

Elizabeth Anne Hin studied poetry formally with George E. Dimock, Richard Wilbur, William Hoover Van Voris, Michael Benedikt, Elizabeth Hardwick, Sir Stephen Spender, and Joseph Brodsky. Her Mother read poetry aloud from *A Child's Garden of Verses* by Robert Louis Stevenson and from other cherished texts from Beth's conception through childhood. Her Father taught her through his admiration for Homer's life, work, and virtuous message, from the world's classics and histories, and from noble and heroic peoples and cultures of all nations. He practiced his faith in the equality of all men and women, and in all aspiration: 'Ad astra per aspera,' ~Seneca. Her Mother was a private living example of this virtue.

Beth has embraced poetry, from reading to writing, since youth, observing in gratitude the poetry infused in sculpture at Wellington's port in New Zealand and attending readings by Jorge Luis Borges at the 92nd Street YMCA in Manhattan, New York, Adrienne Rich in a hallowed hall of Amherst, Massachusetts, Drummond Hadley and Gary Snyder in Anchorage, Alaska, Mary Oliver at a Presbyterian Church in Dallas, Texas. She has been shown kindness in mentoring by writers from John Updike to Carlos Fuentes, Richard Erdoes to Derek Walcott; and by W. S. Merwin, who expressed to her in 1973 that he had written nearly every day since the age of 21, and requested of Beth that she do the same.

## ALSO BY ELIZABETH ANNE HIN

*The Grail: A Story of Issa and Yeshua*, 2014
*Jdg: Poems of Love*, 2016
*Live Oak: Poems of Texas*, 2016
*Willow: Poems of Devotion*, 2016
*Birch: Poems of Love*, 2018
*Thistle: Poems of Life*, 2018

Published by Issa Press, Austin Texas

www.ingramcontent.com/pod-product-compliance
Lightning Source LLC
Chambersburg PA
CBHW031818110426
42743CB00057B/852